**European Colonies in the Americas**

# English Colonies in the Americas

Lewis K. Parker

English Colonies in the Americas
Copyright © 2002 by Rosen Book Works, Inc.

*On Deck*™ Reading Libraries
Published by Rigby
a division of Reed Elsevier Inc.
1000 Hart Road
Barrington, IL 60010-2627
www.rigby.com

**Book Design:** Erica Clendening
**Text:** Lewis K. Parker
**Photo Credits:** Cover, pp. 5, 6, 7 (top), 8–9, 12–13, 15, 16 © NorthWind Picture Archive; p. 4 Erica Clendening; pp. 7 (bottom), 19 © SuperStock, Inc.; p. 11 © Michael Maslan Historic Photographs/Corbis; p. 18, 21 (bottom) © Hulton/Archive/Getty Images; p. 21 (top) © Joseph Sohm, Visions of America/Corbis

All rights reserved. No part of this publication may be reproduced or transmitted in any form or by any means, electronic or mechanical, including photocopying, recording, taping, or any information storage and retrieval system, without permission in writing from the publisher.

*On Deck*™ is a trademark of Reed Elsevier Inc.

11 10
10 9 8
4500228224

Printed in China

ISBN-10: 0-7578-2424-2
ISBN-13: 978-0-7578-2424-1

# Contents

| | |
|---|---|
| Early Settlements | 4 |
| New Colonies | 8 |
| Life in the Colonies | 10 |
| At War | 14 |
| The End of England's Colonies | 18 |
| Glossary | 22 |
| Resources | 23 |
| Index | 24 |

# Early Settlements

England was one of the last European countries to set up colonies in the Americas. The English settlers who came to the Americas wanted to find a better way of life. Some settlers came to practice their religions freely. Other settlers came to find new jobs.

*In 1587, Sir Walter Raleigh (left) helped set up an English colony on Roanoke Island (pictured below) off the coast of present-day North Carolina. Three years later, people bringing supplies to the Roanoke Island colonists found that all of the colonists were gone. To this day, no one knows what happened to the people of the Roanoke colony.*

In 1607, the first lasting English colony was set up at Jamestown, in present-day Virginia. In 1620, English settlers known as Pilgrims started a colony in Massachusetts. They named their settlement Plymouth.

*Life at the Jamestown colony was not easy. The land was poor for farming, and the water was unsafe to drink. Many of the early settlers died from illnesses and lack of food.*

*The Mayflower brought the Pilgrims to Massachusetts. The Pilgrims came to America so they could practice their religion freely.*

The Pilgrims had a hard time during their first year in Plymouth. A Native American named Squanto helped the Pilgrims. He showed them how to plant corn and where to fish. To show their thanks, the Pilgrims had a party for their Native American friends. This gathering of Pilgrims and Native Americans was the first Thanksgiving.

# New Colonies

In 1628, English settlers known as Puritans formed the Massachusetts Bay Colony near present-day Boston.

### The Fact Box

**Between 1663 and 1733, English colonists started settlements in North Carolina, South Carolina, and Georgia.**

*In 1664, England took over the Dutch colony of New Netherland. New Netherland became the English colonies of New York and New Jersey. The Dutch city of New Amsterdam became New York City.*

Within a few years, some of the Puritans left the Massachusetts Bay Colony and started settlements in Connecticut, New Hampshire, Rhode Island, and Maryland.

New York City, 1660s

# Life in the Colonies

Most English settlers in America were farmers. The Middle Colonies had very rich soil. Farmers were able to grow a lot of corn, wheat, and rye. These colonies became known as the Bread Colonies. Farmers sold their crops to other colonists and to people in England.

**The Fact Box**

Philadelphia, New York City, and Boston became the largest cities in the English colonies.

In the New England Colonies, fishing, whaling, and shipbuilding became big businesses.

*Whales were hunted for their blubber, or fat, and bones. The blubber was used to make oil. The bones were used to make jewelry, art, and furniture.*

The Southern Colonies had large farms called plantations.

Tobacco and other crops were sent back to England on ships.

Tobacco, wheat, rice, and indigo were grown on the southern plantations.

*Gathering tobacco, cotton, and other plantation crops was hard work. People from Africa were brought to America to work as slaves on the plantations.*

## At War

From 1754 to 1763, England and France fought over land in North America. The war began when French settlers tried to take English land in the Ohio River Valley. England won the war and took control of Canada and other French lands in the Ohio River Valley.

*George Washington (standing) led English colonists into battle against the French settlers.*

The government in England passed many unfair laws that made life harder for the colonists in America. The laws made colonists pay high taxes on many necessary things, such as sugar, glass, paper, and tea.

Tea was brought to the colonies by ship and was taxed. In 1773, a group of colonists boarded an English ship that was packed with tea. They dumped the tea into Boston Harbor. This act was called the Boston Tea Party.

Colonists were also forced to give English soldiers in the colonies food and places to live. The laws angered the colonists. Colonists wanted to be free from English rule.

## England's Thirteen Colonies in America

| Colony | Date Founded |
|---|---|
| Virginia | 1607 |
| Massachusetts | 1629 |
| Maryland | 1632 |
| Connecticut | 1636 |
| Delaware | 1638 |
| Rhode Island | 1647 |
| North Carolina | 1663 |
| New Jersey | 1664 |
| New York | 1664 |
| New Hampshire | 1680 |
| Pennsylvania | 1681 |
| South Carolina | 1712 |
| Georgia | 1733 |

# The End of England's Colonies

From 1775 to 1783, the colonists fought against England in the Revolutionary War. The colonists won the war and gained their freedom from England. The thirteen English colonies became the United States of America.

*The colonists fought many battles against the English.*

On July 4, 1776, the leaders in England's colonies in America signed the Declaration of Independence.

English became the main language spoken in most of the places that were once English colonies. The laws and practices of England played an important part in the growth of the United States.

## Time Line

| | |
|---|---|
| *1607* | The first lasting English settlement is founded at Jamestown. |
| *1620* | Pilgrims settle in Massachusetts. |
| *1628* | The Massachusetts Bay Colony is formed. |
| *1664* | The Dutch colony of New Netherland becomes the English colonies of New York and New Jersey. |
| *1754–1763* | England and France are at war over land in North America. |
| *1764–1777* | England makes people in its North American colonies pay high taxes. |
| *1775–1783* | The Revolutionary War is fought and England loses control of its colonies in America. |

After the United States gained its independence from England, its leaders wrote the Constitution of the United States. The Constitution explains the main laws and the rights of the American people. The leaders of the United States used ideas from the constitutions and laws of the English colonies in writing the Constitution.

**The Constitution of the United States**

George Washington, an English colonist, fought for freedom from England. He became the first president of the United States of America on April 30, 1789.

# Glossary

**colonists** (**kahl**-uh-nihsts) people who live in a colony

**colony** (**kahl**-uh-nee) a faraway land that belongs to or is under the control of a nation

**declaration** (dehk-luh-**ray**-shuhn) an official, public statement

**harbor** (**hahr**-buhr) a body of water near land where ships dock

**independence** (ihn-dih-**pehn**-duhns) freedom from the control of others

**indigo** (**ihn**-duh-goh) a plant used in making a blue dye

**religion** (rih-**lihj**-uhn) the belief in a god and the practice of praying to that god

**Revolutionary War** (rehv-uh-**loo**-shuh-nehr-ee **wor**) the war fought by the American colonies from 1775 to 1783 to be free from England's rule

**settlement** (**seht**-l-muhnt) a place where people come to live

**settlers** (**seht**-luhrz) people who come to stay in a new country or place

**slaves** (**slayvz**) people who are owned by other people and forced to do work

# Resources

## Books
*The Thirteen Colonies*
by Brendan January
Children's Press (2001)

*The Thirteen Colonies*
by Gail Sakurai
Children's Press (2000)

## Web Site
13 Originals: Founding the American Colonies
http://www.timepage.org/spl/13colony.html

Care was taken in selecting Internet sites. However, Internet addresses can change, or sites can be under construction or no longer exist.

Rigby is not responsible for the content of any Web site listed in this book except its own. All material contained on these sites is the responsibility of its hosts and creators.

# Index

**C**
colonist, 5, 8, 10, 14, 16–18, 21
colony, 4–6, 8, 10, 16–21

**I**
indigo, 13

**M**
Massachusetts Bay Colony, 8–9, 20

**P**
Pilgrims, 6–7, 20
plantations, 12–13
Puritans, 8–9

**R**
religion, 4, 7
Revolutionary War, 18, 20

**S**
settlers, 4, 6, 8, 10, 14